POEMS
Your Boyfriend Should Have
WRITTEN YOU

Bruce Todd LeGrande

POEMS
Your Boyfriend Should Have
WRITTEN YOU

PALMETTO
PUBLISHING
Charleston, SC
www.PalmettoPublishing.com

Copyright © 2023 by Bruce Todd LeGrande

All rights reserved

No portion of this book may be reproduced, stored in a retrieval system, or transmitted in any form by any means–electronic, mechanical, photocopy, recording, or other–except for brief quotations in printed reviews, without prior permission of the author.

Hardcover: 979-8-8229-3468-9
Paperback: 979-8-8229-3404-7

Dedicated to my lovely wife, Lonna.

Contents

MY ANGEL APPEARS	1
BREATH OF FRESH AIR	2
PICKET FENCES	3
MY LIFE BEGAN WITH YOU	4
THE GAMES	5
THE PATH THAT CROSSED	6
LOVING YOU	7
SEEKING HER	8
MORE OF YOU	9
MORE EACH DAY	10
A LOVE UNSURPASSED	11
DEEP FROM WITHIN MY BEING	12
THE HEALING INSIDE	13
LOVES AGONY	14
A SWEET TENDER LOVE	15
LONESOME FOR HIS LOST DOVE	16
THE GENTLE PASSING	17
RUNNING AWAY	18
BIRTHDAY	19
THE SWEET SONGS OF LIFE	20
TO KNOW YOUR HEART	21
ABOUT THE AUTHOR	23

MY ANGEL APPEARS

The cold wind of the early morning put its grip around my neck.
I thought about my present test, feeling I'd been given a stacked deck.
The birds sang their Psalms of a new day as always presiding its way.
I walked to the pond as the sun rose over the trees, christening the day.
The skies were as blue as a heaven could be a tropical paradise.
My mind, reeling with pain and agony, could this life I live suffice?
I came to the edge of the calm waters skin;
I saw a man, tired weary and thin.
I thought of the days when life was serene.
The world was at peace and a beautiful scene.
I peered once again into that water so blue.
An angel appeared and the reflection was you!
I remembered our love, fully tested by time.
Care given with love had grown to a vine.
I knew at that moment my life was complete.
My sweet darling angel, these trials we will beat.
As time passes on, I know there will never be
a day in my life that I won't love you forever!

BREATH OF FRESH AIR

The scent of passion fills the air.
You take it in, but do you dare?
Your mind starts drifting through wonderful places.
The past is gone and so are the faces.
Thrills and wonders engulf your being.
Do you believe what you're really seeing?
I dive into your eyes of crystal blue,
the sun reflecting an awesome hue.
I thought these feelings were gone forever.
Sent to a place of never never.
You've added life to a dimming soul
and brought me life to make me whole.
I will move gently, easy, and true
because the best thing in life is knowing you.

PICKET FENCES

Why must we build these picket fences
and live our lives with such defenses?
I curse the ones that made it that way.
I'll rejoice the moment we finally say
I trust you in all the things that you do.
I know you will love me, all the way through.
The things that were done by those of the past,
I'll wrap the chain, to the sea I will cast.
The moments we spend will be splendid indeed,
the feelings we feel will fulfill every need.
Each time we're apart, a longing will heed.
A time to be close, a life made to lead.
A life that has substance, feelings and truth,
a life that will keep us both in our youth.

MY LIFE BEGAN WITH YOU

I once was a dreamer without any plans.
Looking for comfort, left with empty hands.
I searched for tomorrows, through my stagnated days.
Seeing my life through a dull misty haze.
Suddenly a flower bloomed on a hill,
ingulfing my being and taking my will.
I cried out to God "Could this beauty be mine?"
He said "Yes, my son, it has come your time."
The beautiful flower that I now possess
has given me courage, power, and success.
Her smile is like sunshine, vivid and sweet.
She glows like an angel from her head to her feet.
My love for her is forever, my valentine for life.
I thank you Jesus that she is my wife.

THE GAMES

What is this game the girls like to play?
Stealing men's hearts not missing a day.
They've given men reputations for being this way.
I'm sure many are guilty and someday will pay.
But what is this mysterious ritual of love,
perched like a raven, disguised as a dove.
What is really the truth of this matter;
is love to hurt, heal, or flatter?
We get on our feet to try it again,
opening the gates to let love begin.
This river of love will twist us and bend,
but we'll keep on trying until the end.

THE PATH THAT CROSSED

The mountains we climbed have crumbled to stones.
We look at the wreckage feeling alone.
Stumbling down paths not fulfilling desire,
seeking someone to rekindle the fire.
The choices we made in our past were not true
but written on the pages was someone like you.
You entered my life gently like a leaf in the fall,
resting in my heart greater than anyone at all.
Threading my spirit like a needle and thread,
emptying your passion deep into my head.
Your sensuous ways, your eyes in the nights
send my body to incredible heights.
A young girls way so hard to resist,
reminds me of times of childhood I missed.
Lets open this door of love found anew.
My love, I'm glad that my path crossed with you.

LOVING YOU

You are a sweet summer breeze,
a woman that could bring me to my knees.
Your silent emotions that keep me wondering.
Kissing your lips with my heart thundering.
Caught by the world, I wish I could set you free.
I'll be your friend and help you see
that life is so wonderful, precious and pure.
There is one that will love and heal.
A divine touch from an invisible source
will make you whole and set your course.
My love for you is growing deep.
I hope you feel I'm one to keep.

SEEKING HER

Find me love in this ocean of blue.
Find me someone that will always be true.
Show me eyes that shine in the night.
Chrystal blues beaming magnificent light.
Grant me a touch so gentle to feel.
Give me a love that's awesome and real.
Find me someone to share in my life.
Find me a friend.
Find me a wife.

MORE OF YOU

More of you is all I need;
on thoughts of you my heart will feed.
Warm sunny days, although they're gone,
I'll think of you from dusk to dawn.
Your starlit eyes of an angel before,
she flies through the gates of heavenly doors.
She'll fill my nights and light my days,
throughout my life oh Lord I pray.
Your soft sweet touch and lovely kiss
will always be an awesome bliss.
To find a woman like you is a treasure,
my feelings for you are to great measure.
Please stay with me Dear, we'll love till we're old.
The flowers of love will always unfold.
Filling the valleys with beauty and passion
till we reside in our heavenly mansion.

MORE EACH DAY

I'm awake at three a.m.
You're sleeping so deeply.
I'm rejoicing your name.
It's not that we've bonded together so fine.
It's not that this poem is going to rhyme.
It's not just a phase that I'm going through.
It's not just a thing, it's something that's new.
Your presence is real and a splendor to me.
Your face is a dream, that I finally see.
I love you so much and I love you so deep.
I pray to the Lord that your presence I'll keep.
I think that you know that my love is so true.
How could I hurt you or make you feel blue?
My dear, I love you.
I'll say it again.
You're the one I'll love to the end.

A LOVE UNSURPASSED

Thoughts of the past hindering my sleep
Memories of you and me my mind will always keep.
Feelings of rejection and pain never seem to leave.
Losing the one I really loved is sometimes hard to believe.
Afraid to seek unchartered paths for fear of losing again.
Wondering if I'll be all alone with love never to begin.
But as it is said "Better to have loved then never to have loved at all."
The love that took me to the top has certainly been my fall.
You're easy on the eyes but hard on the heart!

DEEP FROM WITHIN MY BEING

We met with a gentle flow of delight.
Everything special everything right
We soared to the heavens and all boundaries were gone.
Loving the path our lives had been on
My heart moves like thunder to your special ways
No more waiting and counting the days.
You are the one I want to be with
Maybe a pipe dream, but never a myth
My dear, I love you.
I cannot deny.
If you can't see it, I'll never know why.
Sweetheart I vow to always be true.
You'll never be lonely; you'll never be blue.
I'm sorry your past has put up these walls,
I'm praying to God it breaks and it falls.
So, we can be one in this life that is new,
A life that God gave to me and to you.

THE HEALING INSIDE

All master of disguise in our own way
We all run from something, so they say.
Trying to act as if life was so grand,
When deep down inside we could use a hand.
Deep seated memories of passion and pain
Riddle our minds as our hearts become slain.
Bleeding through life with the bandage undone.
Dripping the blood on more than just one
Staining the lives of the one that we love
Searching for peace and hope from above
Gaining the strength to battle the fear.
Finding the one to wipe my tear.
Having the faith to let life take its course.
Trusting forever in the almighty force.

As for me and my house, we will worship the Lord.

LOVES AGONY

An empty heart waits for a filling
Just as love always finds the willing.
The kindhearted patiently wait.
As the unkindly are always late
The thoughts of a lover
Always on the other
The struggle is soft but lightly cutting.
Progressively harder an agonized gutting
The sunshine is there but the rain always comes.
The pain is always present but finally numb.
You walk in the fog wondering why.
Ending the day, you break down and cry.
The faithful will rise in a different way.
They know in their hearts comes a better day.

A SWEET TENDER LOVE

Tender words are all I can say.
My love for you I feel everyday.
Silently taken by your beauty and style
Blue eyes from heaven and a lovely smile
Both of us have had a time in our past
We thought life was true, we thought love would last.
We shared timeless moments together as one.
But memories of the past made us aimlessly run.
I know that someday there may be someone as precious as you.
Forever you will be my friend, forever I will love you.

LONESOME FOR HIS LOST DOVE

I left the one I love on a cold winter day.
My focus on life had long gone away.
Taken by storm in a world so uneasy.
Finding the ways that never would please me.
Hidden inside was a light that was burning.
I didn't know how long I'd been yearning
for someone so special to enter my life.
I never imagined; would this be my wife.
I reach in my heart with daily devotion.
Always to find that sweet, sad emotion
Longing to kiss her and hold her so near.
Whispering sweet words into her ear
I pray for guidance and wisdom to know.
What should I do, where should I go?
Time after time, my love won't diminish,
so maybe it's time to start what we finish.
Even if things don't work out as planned,
I hope in her mind a memory will land.
The dream of a man with passion and love
That ended up losing his one lonesome dove.

THE GENTLE PASSING

The thoughts of me that fill your head
are merely the crust surrounding your bread.
Your love for me could fit in your hand.
I feel in your life, I'm a grain of sand.
Maybe I'm wrong, or seriously blind.
Maybe you need somebody unkind.
I'd give you the world, if it were mine to give.
I would show you a happy life to live.
If this sad filled poem has led to the end
Please know in my heart, you're always my friend
I gave you a spring that was flowing with love.
I guess I was wrong, that it came from above.

RUNNING AWAY

You run from me, and I weep.
Dodging feelings that are so deep
Restless times spent away from you.
Intimate moments I seek are few.
I ran through a field of daisies and dew.
Thrilled with the times of being with you.
But you turned away as if you didn't care.
Leaving me helpless, leaving me bare
I lay on my bed; your fragrance lingers in the air.
Hoping somebody I could be with you where
The stars shine down on you and on me.
A special place that I'd like to be.

BIRTHDAY

Today is your birthday, my beautiful friend.
Each flower you see is the love that I send.
One hundred more birthdays I wish for you, my love.
And one million more blessings from God up above.

THE SWEET SONGS OF LIFE

I wake to the sounds of the birds as they sing.
They sing of a joy of the day that God brings.
Today there's a flower that will come into bloom.
Despite all the sadness of yesterday's gloom
The storms of the past that left her leaves shattered.
Feel now, the sunshine as if nothing else mattered.
The beautiful blossoms that now fill the hillside
Will sprinkle the earth with the hearts that have died.
Bringing new life to a world that was lost.
Praying no mind to whatever the cost
Seeking the future, no boundaries a thought
Teaching the ways, they've finally been taught.

TO KNOW YOUR HEART

I want to know your heart.
If you have some time to spare
As friends to be together
A peaceful time to share.
Your life may seem uprooted.
And somedays be a daze.
But that's what Satan's polluted.
And Christ will begin to raise!

About the Author

Bruce Todd LeGrande hails from the vibrant city of Omaha. A devoted father to five, he recently faced the profound loss of his beloved wife. Amidst the whirlwind of life's triumphs and trials, poetry remained his faithful companion. With his collection, *Poems Your Boyfriend Should Have Written You*, he fulfills a promise to his late wife, sharing a deeply personal narrative of love and heartbreak. His verses extend beyond the page, seeking to touch the hearts of those yearning for love's hope and solace.

www.ingramcontent.com/pod-product-compliance
Lightning Source LLC
LaVergne TN
LVHW041717060526
838201LV00043B/786